This book belongs to

_____

This book is dedicated to my children - Mikey, Kobe, and Jojo.

Ninja Life Hacks™

Hopeful Ninja

By Mary Nhin

Pictures by
Jelena Stupar

"I'm going to fly to the moon one day!" announced Hopeful Ninja.

Hopeful Ninja was very optimistic about her future.

She dreamed big, and more often than not, she would make her dreams come true.

How was she able to do this?

Hopeful Ninja was able to focus on her strengths and find the positives in life, even when things turned upside down.

If she didn't get the class she wanted with all her friends, she looked forward to meeting new people and making additional friends.

When she didn't do so well on her schoolwork, she thought about how much she had improved since the start of the school year.

In her spare time, she loved following stories of people who had failed yet succeeded.

She visualized overcoming obstacles just as they had.

But Hopeful Ninja wasn't always this optimistic.

Once upon a time, the world to her was quite bleak.

If Hopeful Ninja failed at something, she would feel sad and think negative thoughts...

When her parents fought, she would worry and feel guilty...

And her only exposure to people who failed and succeeded was very limited.

But her mindset changed after she was introduced to a great exercise that changed her life forever.

This is what I do to grow a hopeful mindset.
It's called the 3 Fs.
Find the positives.
Focus on our strengths.
Follow success stories.

Find the positives.

Every situation has a silver lining. If we look closely, there's always a positive we can find.

Focus on our strengths.

Instead of looking at what we did wrong, we can choose to focus on what we did right.

Follow success stories.

My favorite way to build hope is to follow success stories. The people we follow can be real living people or people that we read about in books.

Hopeful Ninja thought about what Positive Ninja had said.

It seemed so difficult to change her mindset, but she was determined to be more optimistic.

So she decided to try it.

When the waitress announced they were out of french fries, instead of complaining about it Hopeful Ninja decided to find the positives.

During art hour, she couldn't get her strokes down right, so she focused on her strengths to keep her spirits high.

At home, she went to look for books in the library. She was surprised to find that there were stories of real people who failed, yet succeeded just like her!

One after the other as she followed them, she was transported back in time.

The more Hopeful Ninja practiced the 3 Fs, the more hope it gave her that someday she would accomplish something magnificent too.

Remembering the 3 Fs could be your secret weapon to reach all of your dreams.

Check out our new series Mini Movers and Shakers or
download freebies at ninjalifehacks.tv